Buckinghamshire
Edited by Angela Fairbrace

First published in Great Britain in 2007 by:
Young Writers
Remus House
Coltsfoot Drive
Peterborough
PE2 9JX
Telephone: 01733 890066
Website: www.youngwriters.co.uk

All Rights Reserved

© *Copyright Contributors 2007*

SB ISBN 978-1 84602 965 3

Foreword

Young Writers was established in 1991 and has been passionately devoted to the promotion of reading and writing in children and young adults ever since. The quest continues today. Young Writers remains as committed to the nurturing of poetic and literary talent as ever.

This year's Young Writers competition has proven as vibrant and dynamic as ever and we are delighted to present a showcase of the best poetry from across the UK and in some cases overseas. Each poem has been selected from a wealth of *Little Laureates* entries before ultimately being published in this, our sixteenth primary school poetry series.

Once again, we have been supremely impressed by the overall quality of the entries we have received. The imagination, energy and creativity which has gone into each young writer's entry made choosing the poems a challenging and often difficult but ultimately hugely rewarding task - the general high standard of the work submitted ensured this opportunity to bring their poetry to a larger appreciative audience.

We sincerely hope you are pleased with this final collection and that you will enjoy *Little Laureates Buckinghamshire* for many years to come.

Contents

Ashfold School
Alexander French (10) 1
Angus Haines (10) 1
George Ellison (9) 2
Cameron Hughes (10) 2
Thomas Schmidt (9) 3
Chloe Ranson (9) 3
Oliver Prichard (10) 4
Hannah Fisher (9) 4
Dominic Whaler (10) 5
Emmeline Downie (10) 5
Jack Ellis (10) 6
Ben Hatton (10) 6
Charlie Morris (10) 7
George Kent (10) 7
James Millett (10) 8
Jemima Penfold (9) 9
Lucy Potts (10) 9
Charlie Proctor (9) 10
Robert Skipworth (10) 10
Madeleine Rose (9) 11
James Adams (10) 11
Charlie Williams (10) 12
William Spurgeon (9) 12
Tom Wheeldon (10) 13
Edward Wooster (10) 13
Purdy Sutcliffe (10) 14
Elycia Parker (11) 14
Christopher Wright (9) 15
Jacques Tasker (10) 15
Matthew Cammack (11) 16
Ella Flanagan (10) 16
Camilla Hope (10) 17
Alex Noakes (11) 17
Isabelle Masters (10) 18
Paris Carter (10) 18
Oliver Wright (11) 19
Rebecca White (10) 19
Olivia Batchelor (10) 20

Georgie Currie (10)	20
Bradley Sharp (11)	21
Isabel Taylor (10)	21
Olivia Barlow (10)	22
Toby Czarnota-Bojarski (11)	22
Kelly Davis (11)	23
Charlie Davison (11)	23
Charlie Parker (10)	24
Alicia Green (11)	25
Nicholas Heslop (11)	26
Laura Houghton (11)	26
Joseph Miller-Howes (11)	27
Cameron O'Brien (10)	27
Harry Olive (10)	28
Henry Pringle (11)	28
George Rush (10)	29
Celine Rowley (10)	29
Bethan Sennett (10)	30
Benjamin Spencer (10)	30
Grace DeBanks (11)	31
Max White (10)	31

Aspley Guise Lower School

Tim Mooney (8)	32
Alex Hamling (7)	32
Grace Ludford (9)	32
Tim Jepsen (8)	33
Max Mabey (9)	33
Cara Ramchandani (9)	33
Yvette Wray (7)	34
Oliver Tendler (9)	34
Lucy Tarbox & Niamh Turney (8)	34
Jack Chiappe (8)	35
Alex Giles (9)	35
Ria Emery-King (7)	35
Isabelle Gurney (8)	36
Sophie Toff (7)	36
James Reeder (8)	37
Evie Lewis (7)	37
Lily Ludford (9)	38
Carrick Livingstone (8)	38

Luke Marney (8)	38
Jack Hutchings (7)	39
Kate Thomas (8)	39
Charlotte Grummitt (8)	39
Morgan Tame (8)	40
James Hill (8)	40
Isabel Holland (9)	40
James Lloyd (8)	41

Cadmore End CE Combined School

Taylor Gutteridge (9)	41
Ashley McMahon (8)	41
Jodi Munday (9)	42
Matthew Masterton (8)	42
Daniel Ramsdale (9)	42
Millie-Isabella Ridley (8)	43
Jack Moorin (8)	43
Cameron Bates (7)	43
Hannah Bates (10)	44
Alexander Osypiw (8)	44

Ley Hill School

Elliot Hall (10)	45
James Rolfe (7)	45
Eve Gorst (7)	46
Gavin Davies (7)	46
Jamie Cullen (8)	47
James Asquith (8)	47
Ellie Pardoe (7)	48
Aaron Taylor (7)	48
Tony Sorrenti (7)	49
Mhairi Sanderson (7)	49
Jonathan Shaw (7)	50
Lucia Russell (8)	50
Ashley Davis (10)	51
Chloe Parker (10)	51
Fergus Allan (7)	52
Thomas Dodd (10)	52
Eleanor Cooper (10)	52
Matthew Berry (10)	53
Bethany Sanderson (10)	53

George Loizou (10)	53
Rachel Amankwatia (10)	54
Renny King (10)	54
Elleni Rogers (11)	55
Jenna Taylor (10)	55
Jennifer Davies (10)	56
Kelsi Ellis (10)	56
Roxanne Church (10)	56
Gaby Meek (8)	57
Susie Crabbe (10)	57
Charlotte Rolfe (10)	57
Dominique Puddephatt (8)	58

St Joseph's Catholic Primary School, Chalfont St Peter

Nathaniel Riley (8)	58
Emma Broadley (8)	59
Ella Maher (8)	59
Sean Kennedy (9)	60
Sarah Kay (9)	60
Maggie O'Neill (9)	60
Jessica Chapman (9)	61
Callum Ryan (9)	61
Ciaran Bohan (8)	61
Avneet Kaur Khaira (8)	62
Stephen Moroz (9)	62
Phoebe Roberts (8)	63
Hortense Quazza (9)	63
Katie Schulten (9)	64
Joseph Byrne (9)	64
Cameron Chana (9)	64
Ellie Bees (8)	65
Elizabeth Elsworth (7)	65
Charlotte Gilson (7)	65
Katie McCartney (7)	66
Elena Queally (9)	66
Ladislas Quazza (10)	67
Megan Corrigan (9)	67
Holly Daniels (7)	68
Elizabeth Reeves (7)	68
Alex Wicks (8)	68
Jessica Keyes (7)	69

Victoria Chapman (7)	69
Finlay Burrell (7)	69
Callum Keane (8)	70
Ciara Hildrew (8)	70
Charlie Harrison (7)	71
Evie Vennix (7)	71

St Mary's Wavendon CE Primary School, Wavendon

Amy Werrell (9)	72
Ruby Lockyer (7)	72
Kieran Gissane (10)	72
Liberty Bowler (10)	73
Jake Poyner (10)	73
Courtney McAloon (9)	74

Stoke Poges School

Naveen Mahil (10)	74
Sophie Jones (10)	74
Morgan Pitt (7)	75
Haris Malik (11)	75
Jonathan Schondorfer (11)	75
Nikita Sanan (7)	76
Taylor Nelmes (10)	76
Ryanvir Lalli (10)	77
Munisah Rasheed (10)	77
Zishan Hussain (10)	78
Qasar Ali (10)	78
Stephanie Matthews (10)	79
Nathan Saggar (10)	79
Katie Oakley (10)	80
Elliot Lowe (10)	80
Carol-Anne Smith (10)	80
Fleur Cunningham (10)	81
Rebecca Iona-Smith (10)	81
Ryan Kullar (10)	81
Abigail Duck (10)	82
Sophie Brown (10)	82
Amelia Edwards (10)	82
Nathan Allen (10)	83
Jade Riley (10)	83
Cindy Sidhu (10)	83

Charlie Hall (10)	84
Amie Pearce (10)	84
Poppy Stevens (10)	84
Crispin Imani (9)	85
Sally Hearn (9)	85
Arjan Singh Grewal (9)	85
Megan Wicks (9)	86
Gurneet Dhanoa (10)	86
Sophia Young (9)	87
Charlotte Hough (9)	87
Simran Bains (9)	88
Hemma Jalif (9)	88
Qais Ased Ali (9)	88
Aisha Manzoor (9)	89
Sophie Francis (9)	89
Jasneet Badyal (9)	89
Aisha Afzal (9)	90
Matthew Devine (9)	90
Bethany Johnson (8)	90
Amrita Heer (8)	91
Danni Wylie (9)	91
Azure Jamali (8)	91
Shakeel Pathmanadan (8)	92
Robert Bagge (8)	92
Harley Dyer (7)	93
Josh Stevenson (7)	93
Hanaa Is-haq (7)	94
Simran-Jaya Buttar (8)	94
Iwan Arden (7)	94
Laura Woolhouse (7)	95
Alexa Van Deelen (7)	95
Gareth Forward (7)	95
Max Nowers (8)	96
Khayam Khalid (9)	96
Aisha Anwar (9)	97
Aaron Fetherston (10)	97
Matthew Scott (7)	98

Swanbourne House School

Natalie Pound (9)	98

The Poems

The Death Match

As you enter the heart of football
You see the faithful roaring crowd.
You don't realise what's happened or what's happening.
You just think it's a friendly between two rivals.
As the match starts you see the metal fence,
You see the people dying and then you realise,
This is no friendly, this is life and death.
You see the people crying, crying over dead.
This is no joke; this is a game of life and death.
You can't choose, you can't lie, you can only hope to survive.
This is famous, this is the match,
The match that killed the thousands and was friends with Death.

Alexander French (10)
Ashfold School

Golden Hair

Your yellow stream of golden hair
Runs down the back of your elegant head
Untangling, waving, weaving itself around
Simmering in the light making everyone blind
Your golden hair sways as you walk
It sways like a beehive on a branch
As your hair slowly drifts down
Lightly you lie on your soft pillow.
Your yellow stream of golden hair.

Angus Haines (10)
Ashfold School

Don't Forget To Eat Your Veg

I go to this school that I think is really cool
And the school dinners are dinners not from your lunch box
We get lasagne, Bolognese, fish and chips
All hot food but sometimes cold
Yummy, yummy, mouth-watering, lick your lips.

Don't forget your veg now, five a day, five a day,
Peas, potatoes, carrots, and courgettes
Broccoli, baked beans give you wind I bet!

Next comes pudding, dessert or sweet,
Call it what you want but it can't be beat,
We get apple pie, apple crumble, jelly and ice cream,
You can keep the rice pudding so take it please
Treacle tart is the best, you know what I mean.

Don't forget your veg now, five a day, five a day,
Peas, potatoes, carrots and courgettes,
Broccoli, baked beans give you wind I bet!

George Ellison (9)
Ashfold School

London

London's always a beautiful place,
Theatres always really full,
Taxis cost a fortune,
Kids eating lots of food,
Kids get up to no good,
The fights between Chelsea and Man U,
Never end up in much good,
Wembley stadium being built,
The prop goes into the Mall,
The hustlers have the Queen's jewels.

Cameron Hughes (10)
Ashfold School

Animals

Animals are beautiful but the big ones sometimes roar,
You'll have to get used to it because they'll do it even more.
Some are cute and small but others are very big and tall.
Some of them live in caves and don't bother with a door.
Mice and cats, dogs and maybe rats are pets,
But then that means you have to take them to the vets.
Lions, monkeys, tigers and bats, they could kill you just like *that!*
Animals live in woods, jungles, farms (or in other words a barn)
Some sleep at night, some in the day and some sleep in piles of hay.
Animals get clean by licking themselves, humans have washes in foam,
But I'm afraid that's the end of my poem!

Thomas Schmidt (9)
Ashfold School

Chocolate, Chocolate

Yummy, yummy in my tummy
Chocolate is so very scrummy.
Plain, dark, white and milk
Many flavours just like silk.
I love them all, big and small
If only it could make me tall.
Easter bunnies in a nest
Smuggling bars of Galaxy
Which let's face it, is the best!
Yummy, yummy in my tummy
Chocolate is so very scrummy!

Chloe Ranson (9)
Ashfold School

Guitar

All the six different strings play different sounds.
All you could dream of is ripping those rock strings all around.
It feels like you're jumping into a pop cloud.
God, I just wish I was allowed.

Oliver Prichard (10)
Ashfold School

Monsters

I dread the night
And the moon and stars
For Mum to pull my curtains
And Dad to go to the bar.

But when all this happens
I run upstairs to bed
I slam open the wooden door
Right onto little Ted.

If there was a monster
Hidden behind the door
It would be squashed like a pancake
But now there is the floor.

The floor's a sea of comics
And tiny little Teds
But there could be a monster
Right under my bed.

And then I feel the urge
To take a flying leap,
I land safely on my bed
Phew! I'm safe to sleep!

Hannah Fisher (9)
Ashfold School

Athletics

Athletics is a sport that you just want more
But some people think it is a bore.
As runners whizz past, you think you're number one
But as you try to catch up, the race is already won.

Dominic Whaler (10)
Ashfold School

The Fruit Sherbet

There is a whirr going through me
I feel so strange
It's like a volcano's about to explode inside me
Crack, snap, crack, snap, pop!
The bag has burst
Thud, thud, thud, sweets are falling like hail.

It looks like a little pink boat striped with a darker shade
It's floating on its clear, wrapping river
I sniff
It's not a boat anymore
But a large fruit bowl filled to the brim ready to be eaten.

I run my finger along the surface
It's like a stretch of bark
Rough in some places and smooth in others.

My time has come
I have to eat it
I'm going to eat it
Creamy, delicate, fizzing
A taste to last a lifetime
Crunch!
There's more surprises lurking in the inside
Sherbet frazzling in my mouth
Sour and delicious
Sherbet fruits are the best!

Emmeline Downie (10)
Ashfold School

The Fruit Sherbet

Excited and jubilant
So crackling, so snappy
Creamy green with smooth strips
Must grab violently, need to tear open
Stupendous urges to unwrap came, *crunch, snap,* it was unwrapped.

Then the smells came
The heavenly smells like sweet sugar
It was sticky and like paradise
It was irrestible
It was in my mouth
A sweet fizzy assault of fizzzz which never ends . . .

Jack Ellis (10)
Ashfold School

Fruit Sherbet

Frenzied,
Hungry,
Crackling, crunchy bag,
Sweet, oval-shaped,
All wrapped up in clear paper!

I am so very tempted,
Snappy, crackly, poppy,
I just can't stand the temptation,
I have to! I have to!
The fruity sugary smell is too good for me!

It is so good and sticky,
I must keep the stickiness on my fingers forever,
It tastes just like I've gone to Heaven,
Full of sweetness,
My mouth must burst into pieces!

Ben Hatton (10)
Ashfold School

Fruit Sherbet

Jolly
Hungry
Crackly
Noisy!
A wrapper with a lovely red covering of strawberry.
Eventually, I wanted to grab it
And unwrap it
And eat it!
I unwrapped it and heard the crackling sound.
It smelt like the great taste of cotton candy.
It felt like a dream come true.
It tasted like a great flower of fruity strawberry.
I want my mouth to taste like it all the time!
I had an amazing attack of sherbet in my mouth.

Charlie Morris (10)
Ashfold School

Fruit Sherbet

Gleeful.
Grasping.
Crackly and noisy.
Pink with white stripes.
Urgent and excited about eating this pink cuboid!
It smells like all my dreams come true.
It feels sticky and I feel like I am going to Heaven.
A yummy scrummy sweet.
I want this taste to go on forever.

George Kent (10)
Ashfold School

Fruit Sherbet

Excited, that is my feeling now.
The bag opens . . .
I hear a crackly snap.
My feelings are to pounce,
I can't resist the urge to dive in for the sherbet.

I see the sherbet.
I really feel peckish.
It is green with sheets of white powered sherbet dust.
That's when I feel the tingle of Heaven,
The wrapper twisted like a rope.

When I feel the wrapper, I feel flatness and softness of plastic,
I really want to open it now as my mouth waters.

I get the slightest sniff, lime!
It's so tempting,
I just want to eat it.
The sniff,
A whole flow of the lime smell goes through my nose and sort of stays there.
I just can't get my nose away from it.

Then I touch it, it feels so good and sticky.
Perfect, even the touch is better than the smell.
It sort of has the sticky sensation of paradise.

It tingles in my mouth as I keep it in, the flavour stays.
I want this flavour to never leave me.
It makes me feel like collapsing because the taste is so relaxing.
A wave of fizz goes through my mouth, like thunder eating it away and then . . .
Boom!
That's the end of my sherbet.

James Millett (10)
Ashfold School

Fruit Sherbet

Thoughtful
Hungry
Crackly
Stripy pinkie
Urgent
Grab it
Strip it
Shove it in my mouth!

Hands tingling
Mouth watering
Wrapper scraping
So refreshing and strawberry
Like a magnetic fruit
Oh that rough feeling, long and juicy like I had never tasted before.

A solid rock
All rigid, crunchy and fizzy
Then I get attacked by a sour and soft feeling.
Why does this have to end?

Jemima Penfold (9)
Ashfold School

Fruit Sherbet

Excited
Tingly
Crunchy
Rough
Luscious green
A dainty wrapper
So tempting to grab, unwrap and stuff in my mouth.
My hands are shaking, I must eat it.
It's the greatest smell of lime ever, rigid but sticky.
It tastes fruity, I feel relieved that it's in my mouth.
So sour and fizzy, I never want this to stop.

Lucy Potts (10)
Ashfold School

Fruit Sherbet

Happy and excited
Hungry
Noisy and crackly
Glimmering, shining purple and green wrapping.
Eat it
Grab it
Lunge on it
Pounce on it
Rigid wrapper
Smells of the sweet
I am hungrier than ever before.
It smells like all of the dreams in the world.
It feels sticky and bumpy.
It tastes like Heaven.
I wish it would stay with me forever.
Charlie Proctor (9)
Ashfold School

Fruit Sherbet

It looks so yummy,
The crackling of the wrapper
Small and purple, it looks
So good, so tasty,
So mouth-watering.

It's refreshing, it's lovely,
It feels sugary, it feels sticky.
The blueberry taste,
I feel so hungry.
Robert Skipworth (10)
Ashfold School

Fruit Sherbet

Happy, hungry, crackly, snappy
A shiny wrapped sherbetty treat.
Hard and smooth, pink and oval
With little white stripes around it.

Urging to eat this delicious surprise!
I picked up the sweet.
Suddenly I rolled it about
Immediately I opened it!

A mouth-watering sweet,
It smelt so fruity, I could not resist.
It tasted like a real peach,
Sticky to the touch - a delicious delight!

It tasted like the best thing I've ever tasted!
A peach, mouth-watering surprise!
It fizzed, fizzed, fizzed!
It crunched, crunched, crunched!
It clattered all around my mouth.

Madeleine Rose (9)
Ashfold School

The Globe

The past
Has come to me
The year 1596
I am acting at the Globe Theatre in London
Shakespeare's special theatre
People call it the Wooden O
But it's hard to believe it's made of wood
It's too beautiful.

James Adams (10)
Ashfold School

Shakespeare's Globe

S hakespeare's Globe
H ollow and round
A ctors singing a nicely tuned sound
K ingly actors dancing and singing
E yes drawn to the stage as the bell starts ringing
'S hh,' says the fairy
P rancing around being scary
E vening is now with
A *pop* and a *pow*
R ain and more rain
E vil witches casting pain.

Charlie Williams (10)
Ashfold School

Fruit Sherbet

Frenzied.
Crinkly
Snappety
A floating shape, a yellow Heaven
A world of glace fruit.

I've unwrapped it with care,
Tempting, tempting,
I might explode
Lemon
Fruity
Tangy
Sticky
Eat
me

In my mouth

Fizz

Crackle

Gulp.

William Spurgeon (9)
Ashfold School

Fruit Sherbet

Thrilled
Hungry
Crackling and popping
Sweet, sumptuous and delicious, orange chunk of goodness.

I am urged to rip off the wrapper and suck until it is no more.
As I am taking the wrapper off, the fruit sherbet turns slowly,
I want to pounce,
It smells like freshly picked oranges covered in sugar.

Sticky, sugary,
I have to eat it *now!*
I feel so . . . so calm.

It tastes of an orange sugar-coated ball melting in my mouth.
A burst of sherbet goodness.
When I crunch, it's so wonderful
I don't want it to stop.

Tom Wheeldon (10)
Ashfold School

Fruit Sherbet

Happy, excited.
Crackly and noisy.
Green, yellow and also stripes.

Pounce on it, then tear like a cat.
It sounds like a vibration, tinkling
into my hand, but now I really want to eat it!

It smells like a lemon and everything in the world.
It feels sticky and it feels like I'm in Heaven.
It tastes sherbetty, sweet and e x t r a o r d i n a r y!

I really want to keep this taste forever and ever.
Amen!

Edward Wooster (10)
Ashfold School

Fruit Sherbet

A crackling, scraping bag
Smooth, shiny, sparkly, clear
Green like the swaying trees
A perfectly rounded cuboid
Timid and tempted
I need to pounce and rip the wrapper
But then I gently open it
Listening for people behind me.

Like the sherbet from Heaven
It gives off creamy apple tastes
Sticky toffee but yet it's not
Smooth as silk, a fruit sensation
I feel faint-headed
The taste is so good
Sparkly and sweet
A wave of sherbet fizzing, buzzing
Please don't leave me
Oh that taste!
Five . . . four . . . three . . . two . . . one . . . it's gone!
I'm back down to Earth with a *smack!*

Purdy Sutcliffe (10)
Ashfold School

The Wooden O

S himmering in the moonlit river
H allowed out like a wooden O
A live with all sorts of smells
K eeping secrets from the unclean eye
E cstatic people from near and far
S tand and listen hard
P rancing around upon the stage
E ven forgetting about the plague
A fter the performance comes to an end
R ich people descend
E xiting this strange world again!

Elycia Parker (11)
Ashfold School

Fruit Sherbet

Tired, exhausted and hungry.
I hear crunching, banging and crackling.
I see a purple jewel in a wrapper,
My mouth is watering,
I must eat the sweet.
I can smell the lovely fruity smell of blackcurrant.

It is sticky, as sticky as superglue.
It doesn't feel sticky anymore
And the yummiest thing in the world is coming to my mouth.
I must not crunch it because I want the taste to last forever.

Christopher Wright (9)
Ashfold School

Fruit Sherbet

Tired
Hungry
I've seen a fruit sherbet bag
It's a crunchy, crackling thing
I've taken a sweet out
It's a shiny orange stripy block
I feel excited, tempted, I must eat it!
My mouth's watering
I smell it; it is a great smell, just like orange
Now I really must gobble it up
It feels sticky
Please, I must gulp it down
I eat it
It is mouth-watering
It must have more
I crunch it, it tastes great
It is the fizzy, tasty sherbet.

Jacques Tasker (10)
Ashfold School

The Actor's Feelings

Watching the crowd
Over the edge of stage
Overexcited
Dazzled by performance
Eating and drinking
Nasty rotten things
Only, nothing was there.
Only in my mind I was seeing these people
Finding that actually it is quite scary.
Prancing and dancing
Leaping and lying
All of them fun
Yet not . . .
Satisfying.

Matthew Cammack (11)
Ashfold School

The Actor's Riddle

S mells surrounding the actors
H atred from the hounds of Hell
A t the Globe in Shakespeare's time
K eep the plays going
E ver-speaking
S howing their men like women
P leasure from the actors came
E ver-singing
A round the stage they glide
R eassured by drunken cheers
E ver-acting
S howing off their talents

G etting changed behind the scenes
L ost for words
O ver the stage
B reaking free from the heavens
E xcitement rising from the crowd.

Ella Flanagan (10)
Ashfold School

The Feeling Of Time At The Globe

Slowly but carefully I walked through the door
I stood, I gazed as the stage appeared in front of me
Everything was too much!
The smell, the atmosphere, everything
I fell, I felt sick.

I was in Shakespeare's Globe in 1600,
It was as if I had travelled back on a timeline.
The actors on the most amazing stage,
The poorer people drinking beer down below in the pit,
The richer people crowding into the floors above me,
Gazing as the royalty gracefully stepped onto the balcony
                                        above the stage.

Slowly, I walked through the crowds,
The odd shout across the theatre.
I started to feel dizzy and sick again
As if being pulled very tightly through a very small hole.
I started dropping, dropping, it was going on forever.

I landed back on the stage in the modern Globe,
It felt so quiet, so empty.
From then on I was the one with the amazing feeling in the Globe.

Camilla Hope (10)
Ashfold School

Life At The Globe

W ild excitement fills your heart
O verlooking where those groundlings stood
O riginal words of Shakespeare art
D enying everything's made of wood
E cstatic feeling from heavens above
N asty devils from Hell below

O verall it comes together with love seeing everything now you know.

Alex Noakes (11)
Ashfold School

Shakespeare's End, But Beginning

The crippled man writing constantly in his baggy pantaloons
With the same quill scratching away at the parchment.
His profession growing every time his plays succeed
Whilst the candle flickers in the dark, dusty room.
He thinks, he thinks of his other plays.
The lines swirling round his head, like a load of bright twinkling stars
                                                in the dark night sky.
He falls to the floor, the quill drifting out of his hands.
The candle goes out, his heart lifts.
He realises that it's only the beginning of a new Shakespeare.

Isabelle Masters (10)
Ashfold School

The Globe Theatre

G reat day
L ifts from Hell
O ut comes the Devil
'B ah!' he says
E yes glistening

T he voices go quiet
H eavens open as
E veryone cheers
A nd angels fly down
T rick tables come in
R egally the dukes show off
E veryone's excited.

Paris Carter (10)
Ashfold School

The Globe Theatre

W ow, it's amazing, beautiful; I thought in my head
    I could hear cheering
O utside the Globe is beauty too and like the endless stage
O n the stage is astounding, you can imagine cheering as your
    play has ended
D rag your feet up the stairs into the Globe's rafters, fire the cannon
    the play has started, the crowd begins to see
E ngage your audience in what you have in store for them
N ow the play has ended and you go off feeling good

O ff with the clothes of former Shakespeare stars.

Oliver Wright (11)
Ashfold School

A Super Day At The Globe Theatre

G o to the Globe
L ots of magical fun!
O f watching plays
B etter ones are always done
E very day at the Globe

T he theatre's absolutely amazing!
H earing is rather hard
E ars are listening, eyes are gazing
A t actors and the ones high up at
T he groundlings sounding like a yard!
R emember the plays you go to watch there
E veryone loves the things they see there.

Rebecca White (10)
Ashfold School

The Globe Theatre Poem

G oing to the Globe is always
L ooking beautiful
O ver the hills
B ack to the olden days
E ven I will never forget when I went to the Globe

T he angels fly down from Heaven
H appy time has come again
E very time you go there you will love it more
A nd more
T he devils jump out of Hell
R ousing up a mighty roar to scare all the groundlings
E nemies of the angels!

Olivia Batchelor (10)
Ashfold School

The Globe Theatre

G roundlings stand upon the rushes
L owest of the lot
O verhead the richer folk sit
B ut without the view of the actors
E ntertaining the gigantic crowd

T he Globe standing high and tall
H ere in London town
E very day there are new plays so
A ctors are forever acting and
T he Wooden O is forever producing plays such as
R omeo and Juliet
E rrors or Henry VIII.

Georgie Currie (10)
Ashfold School

Shakespeare's Poem

S mell the groundlings from high above the five-foot stage
H ell is somewhere below as witches and demons are summoned
A ppear to strike or kill important people like Macbeth
K ings, queens, angels, gods but always appear from Hell
E ntering like a shadow on a midsummer morning
S uddenly flying off the stage of going to Hell
P eacefully going in and out of the theatre
E xiting like a pack of hounds on the hunt
A bove the angels helping God
R eappearing like demons on a hunt
E xpecting the crowd to shout and cheer.

Bradley Sharp (11)
Ashfold School

A Weird Thing That Happened

S enses tell me I'm in the past
H ow the heavens open
A ngels flying down from Heaven
K eeping the Globe Theatre safe and sound
E ven the smells are different here
S eeing the buildings gazing down
P assing through the theatre
E verywhere seems different
A nd then I see a man looking around
R ummaging through some papers
E veryone else stares at him, his name is Shakespeare!

Isabel Taylor (10)
Ashfold School

The Globe Theatre

The wonderful theatre,
The wonderful Globe,
The fabulous man who played right here.

Shakespeare's the man,
The only one that can
Write a very good story plan.

The play's starting,
Hip hip *hooray!*
What's it going to be today?

The horrid smells,
The ghastly shouts,
'Be quiet down there you stinky lot!'

The posh up above,
The peasants down below
And all of us in the middle row.

The play's ended,
Cheer! Clap!
What a wonderful performance here at the Globe!

Olivia Barlow (10)
Ashfold School

Shakespeare's Poem

S hakespeare, king of the theatre
H amlet, one of his tales
A ntony and Cleopatra, both dead souls
K ing Macbeth has slain a man
E vermore will Hermia and Lysander be together
S tratford where William was born
P uck, the mischievous fairy
E geus, the father of Hermia
A thens is ruled by Theseus
R etiring rooms where actors rest
E nding, another way of saying over.

Toby Czarnota-Bojarski (11)
Ashfold School

Globe Theatre Daydream

G lowing lights, shouting loud
L aughing crowd, not a sound
O nly a scream and shout
B ecause the actor is a lout
E ating oranges to cover up the smell

T he witches have just cast a spell
H alf a moon is up in the sky
E veryone must say goodbye
A fter a night of fabulous fun
T he theatre is good and done
R oyalty has locked up
E arthly beings have risen up

D ark has come, the night is young
A ll evil has also come
Y elling has disappeared
D eathly creatures have reappeared
R ealm of evil has begun
E ating oranges has been done
A ll of night is simply old
M en have toiled and sold their gold.

Kelly Davis (11)
Ashfold School

Globe Theatre Poem

S hakespeare, king of shadows
H amlet, king of his Denmark
A ny day there was a play
K eep his scripts out in the world
E xplain his show to someone new
S unny sunshine plays all day
P owerful performances every day
E xtra pay for one nice cushion
A ntony, enemy of Cleopatra
R ipping voices spread round the globe
E vil spirits are near, beware the witches are near.

Charlie Davison (11)
Ashfold School

The Globe Theatre

The atmosphere around you
The times coming back
The thatched roof and the decorated stage
Marble pillars with wall hangings flopping down
The glistening eyes watching in the moonlight
Actors dressed as angels dropping from the heavens.

Richard III
Hamlet
Romeo and Juliet
The full crowd staring in amazement
Backstage candlelit room with the actors waiting for their cue
The stage high
The actors standing tall and powerful

But people still talk over the plays
But now silence
No giant crowds
No old-fashioned clothing
Only modern tourists and visitors looking around
Not as many plays
Not as many people
The Globe Theatre is empty.

Charlie Parker (10)
Ashfold School

A Journey Of The Globe

In a puff of smoke the witch appears,
The witch appears who everyone fears.
Out of the trapdoor in the floor,
She will stay evil for evermore.
People come from far and wide,
From city and street and countryside
To see Macbeth at the Globe.

It has no roof; it's wooden and white,
The O in the roof gives the theatre its light.
Rich in the balconies, poor on the ground,
Unlike now the theatre's full of sound.
Sweaty and stinky the peasants stand,
Then into the cauldron the witches put sand.
People eat oranges to cover the smell,
No one's healthy, no one's well.

Plays are not put on in the night,
Because the O doesn't give its light.
The government hate the plays and this place,
With all the dresses covered with lace.
People rejoice shout and sing,
All the churches let their bells ring.
Because they love the Globe.

Alicia Green (11)
Ashfold School

Macbeth And The Three Witches

Back from the battle, Macbeth rides
Through village, hamlet and countryside.
Three witches appear in a gloomy dark grove,
And it's to that grove that Macbeth rode.
'Macbeth, Thane of Glamis!' the first witch cried,
'Yes, that is me,' Macbeth tried.
'Macbeth, Thane of Cawdor!' the second witch shouted,
His valiant steed, Macbeth mounted.
Just as he was about to ride
'Macbeth, King of Scotland!' the third witch cried.

Nicholas Heslop (11)
Ashfold School

Shakespeare Poem

S hakespeare, king of stories
H amlet, one of his many plays,
A von, the river which he lived by
K illing, his plays were mainly based on
E verlasting fame for evermore
S phere-shaped was the Globe
P lays he was famous for
E njoyment the Globe Theatre
A musement for everyone
R ight, his plays were mostly correct
E veryone went home as happy as can be.

Laura Houghton (11)
Ashfold School

That Theatre Day

Groundlings were letting off the worst smell yet
Drunk people upstairs were making a bet
All the actors put on a play
No one was quiet that theatre day
I watched Macbeth, the witches were bad
Midsummer Night's Dream made everyone sad
The rich people chattered, the groundlings all howled
Nobody was quiet as the witches prowled
That was the end of my theatre day
I had a brilliant first of May.

Joseph Miller-Howes (11)
Ashfold School

Globe Theatre Poem

S hakespeare, king of shadows
H amlet, king of Denmark
A ntony, enemy of Cleopatra
K ing of plays
E vil are the three witches
S hakespeare's famous Globe
P illars that hold the stage roof so high
E xtra pay for one nice cushion
A fter nightfall his plays don't get seen
R adical plays shown during the day
E ating in the pit has stopped.

Cameron O'Brien (10)
Ashfold School

Waiting For A Play

S hakespeare, he's the man
H amlet, king of Denmark
A pplause from the crowd
K night in the balcony
E nded by a play, done by amateurs
S mells all around
P eople creating atmosphere
E ating stale bread
A ll waiting
R oar the cannon fires
E nd, people walk home happy, as happy can be.

Harry Olive (10)
Ashfold School

The Globe Theatre

In the theatre
On the stage
The feeling's the same
Gobsmacked, amazed, astonished, scared
You must have cared
The stage walked all around you
Pulling you in
Letting go of your skin
The dog waves its legs in the air
When fighting a bear
There you go
There's my say
Just go to the theatre, anyway.

Henry Pringle (11)
Ashfold School

Shakespeare

S hakespeare, king of shadows
H amlet, a king within his play
A nother king, Macbeth his name
K nowledge that was a gem for his age
E ffortless writing of plays is pure
S ite on which the Globe is placed, next to the beautiful River Thames
P owerful performances happened every day
E arl of Cambridge - a brave man, conspiring against the king
A nticipation, everybody waits for the performance
R ound the theatre, round you go
E ager to go, no way!

George Rush (10)
Ashfold School

Shakespeare's Globe

S hakespeare, king of the theatre
H appy and heroic
A lcohol and noise
K in and all your peers
E nemies of the men who act
S houting out to the audience
P leading too, the storylines
E xcellent costumes as well as the scripts
A pplauding, the sound that comes in speech
R ich and poor, fun for all
E vil are the Macbeth witches
S olid painted, marble oaks

G athering of groups of friends
L aughing loudly at the words
O verall a good performance
B eautiful is the theatre
E vening is over and everything is done.

Celine Rowley (10)
Ashfold School

The Heart Of Shakespeare And The Globe

Shakespeare, the one we love
His writing flows like a dove
In the midnight sky we will always see his shadow
Round the park or somewhere narrow
One day the Globe was found
To perform plays, it was so interestingly round
The day of my trip I was filled with joy
I couldn't believe a girl had to be played by a boy!
I will always come back to find out some more
And I will admire Shakespeare for evermore.

Bethan Sennett (10)
Ashfold School

Shakespeare Poem

S hakespeare
H amlet his best
A lways there was a play
K ing of shadows he was
E xciting actors there were
S unny dreamy days there were plays
P erformances he wrote
E xtra actors for him
A ctors came to him
R arely his plays were missed
E arly plays were always there.

Benjamin Spencer (10)
Ashfold School

The Globe Theatre

S is for Shakespeare, king of the shadows
H is for Hamlet, king of his plays
A is for anxious people
K is for keener they get while they wait
E is for excitement as the play starts
S is for sudcenly something appears
P is for peanuts sold to eat
E is for enthusiasm from all actors
A is for action as the death scene comes around
R is for romance, two or more lovers
E is for ending, everyone is sad but they all wait for
                              the arrival of a new one!

Grace DeBanks (11)
Ashfold School

Shakespeare Around The Globe

S cripts he wrote
H appiness that his plays brought
A pplause that he received
K ids that watched his plays
E ncouragement that he got from the audience
S illy gags in his plays
P ieces of fruit were thrown at the actors
E xcitement all around the theatre
A trapdoor, up and down
R ebuilding the Globe
E nd of poem, end of Shakespeare.

Max White (10)
Ashfold School

First Flame

In a dark icy town there grew a cliff.
Below the cliff there lay a road.
Beyond the road there crept a field.
Beyond the field there flowed a river.
Beside the river there slept a rock.
Under the rock there breathed an egg.
In the egg burst a flame
And from that flame there was dragon birth.

Tim Mooney (8)
Aspley Guise Lower School

Dragon Birth

In a massive mouldy mountain there was a rock.
Beneath the rock there was a tunnel.
In the tunnel there was an egg.
In the egg there was a dragon.

Alex Hamling (7)
Aspley Guise Lower School

Dragon Birth

On the edge of a cliff there was a hole
Beneath the hole there was a nest.
In the nest there was an egg
On the egg there was a crack.
From the crack there was a leg
From the leg dragon came.

Grace Ludford (9)
Aspley Guise Lower School

Dragon Birth

In a dangerous great snowstorm there stood a mountain.
In the mountain a hole lay still.
Inside that hole a rock lay.
Behind the rock there floated an egg.
In that egg there formed a crack.
From that crack a dragon came.

Tim Jepsen (8)
Aspley Guise Lower School

Dragon Birth

In the high mountain there sat a nest.
In the nest there lay an egg.
In the egg there was a crack.
From that crack there was a flame.
From that flame a dragon came.

Max Mabey (9)
Aspley Guise Lower School

Dragon Birth

In a big wide desert there was a plant.
Behind the plant there stood a pole.
Inside the pole there dripped some sand.
In the sand there lay a nest.
In the nest there slept an egg.
In that egg there came a crack
And from that crack dragon came.

Cara Ramchandani (9)
Aspley Guise Lower School

Dragon Birth

In a blue sea there stood a hole
And around that hole there floated sand worms
And near those sand worms there lay an egg.
The egg had a crack in it
And then a flame burst through and then dragon came.

Yvette Wray (7)
Aspley Guise Lower School

Dragon Birth

In a tree there lay a nest
And on that nest there lay an egg
And in that egg there slept a slimy dragon
And one day later the egg cracked
And then burst out a dragon!
What came out of that dragon was a glow and a burst of fire!

Oliver Tendler (9)
Aspley Guise Lower School

Gelert Kennings

Bone stealer
Garden runner
Tail twitcher
Ear flicker
Eye blinker
Baby waker
Wolf chaser
Sword greeter
Nose wriggler
Blood dripper
Dog sneezer
Friend maker
Death arriver.

Lucy Tarbox & Niamh Turney (8)
Aspley Guise Lower School

Dragon Birth

Above the rocky ocean there sat a cliff.
On that cliff there sat a fire.
Beside the fire there lay a nest.
In the nest waited an egg.
The egg began to crack then out of the egg there burst a flame
And after that, dragon came!

Jack Chiappe (8)
Aspley Guise Lower School

Dragon Birth

In the cold, dark night wood there was a tree.
By the tree there was a leaf.
Under the leaf there was some soil.
By the soil there were some insects.
Under the insects was an egg
And in the egg was a crack.
By the crack was some fire
And by that fire was a *dragon!*

Alex Giles (9)
Aspley Guise Lower School

Dragon Birth

In the dry, cold mountain,
There stood a black hole.
Beneath the dark hole stood an egg.
And in that egg a crack waited.
In the crack was a flame.
From the flame a dragon came.

Ria Emery-King (7)
Aspley Guise Lower School

Dragon Birth

In the roaring seaside there stood a cliff.
In the cliff there was a hole.
In the hole there were some roses.
Beneath the roses there was a box
And in the box there was an egg.
From the egg came some smoke.
From the smoke came a pitch of fire
And from that fire dragon came!

Isabelle Gurney (8)
Aspley Guise Lower School

Gelert Kennings

Baby protector
Nose twitcher
Garden runner
Wolf chaser
Tail wagger
Bone cruncher
Animal chaser
Rabbit chaser
Deer slayer
Ear twitcher
Wolf slayer
Cry maker
Sword meeter
Death greeter.

Sophie Toff (7)
Aspley Guise Lower School

Gelert Kennings

Wolf fighter
Tail shaker
Deer hunter
Heaven greeter
Baby protector
Wolf fighter
Great hunter
Wind liker
Brave hunter
Deer finder
Wolf killer
Sword meeter.

James Reeder (8)
Aspley Guise Lower School

Gelert Kennings

Babysitter
Cry maker
Bone cruncher
Bone stealer
Rabbit killer
Wolf fighter
Animal sniffer
Sorry meeter
Sword greeter
Angel arriver
Garden runner.

Evie Lewis (7)
Aspley Guise Lower School

Dragon Birth

In a hot, fiery volcano there was a lava pool.
Beneath the pool there was a nest.
In the nest there was a bee's home.
Beneath the bee's home there was a cliff.
In the cliff there was an egg
And in that egg there was a crack.
From that crack there was a flame.
From that flame there was a fire
And from that fire dragon came.

Lily Ludford (9)
Aspley Guise Lower School

Dragon Birth

In a cliff there was a hole
And in that hole there lay a stone
And under that stone there grew an egg
And in that egg a flame came
And from that flame came a fire
And from that fire, dragon came.

Carrick Livingstone (8)
Aspley Guise Lower School

Dragon Birth

In the wild, wet forest there sat a hole.
In the hole there lay a stone.
Under the stone there cracked an egg.
In the egg lay a dragon.
By the dragon sparkled a sword.

Luke Marney (8)
Aspley Guise Lower School

Dragon Birth

In a dangerous forest there was a hole
And in that hole there was a dark tunnel
And in that tunnel there was a speck of light
And that speck of light looked like a flame
And from that flame a dragon came
And that dragon was really *big!*

Jack Hutchings (7)
Aspley Guise Lower School

Dragon Birth

There was a deserted castle.
In the castle there was a big echoey dungeon
And in the dungeon there stood a table
And on the table there was a cage.
In the cage there wobbled an egg.
From the egg a dragon came.

Kate Thomas (8)
Aspley Guise Lower School

Gelert Kennings

Baby protector
Wolf killer
Animal hunter
Wolf hunter
Heart breaker
Sword greeter
Happy smiler.

Charlotte Grummitt (8)
Aspley Guise Lower School

Dragon Birth

In the dark, dark castle there creaked a dungeon.
In the dungeon lay a pile of weapons.
Under the weapons lay an egg
And in that egg was a flame
And out of the flame came a dragon.

Morgan Tame (8)
Aspley Guise Lower School

Grew An Oak

In the wild, wet wood there grew an oak.
Beneath the oak there lay a cave
And in that cave the moss crept.
Beneath the moss there was a stone.
Beneath the stone there lay an egg
And in that egg there crept a crack.
From that crack there came a flame.
From the flame there flew a fire
And from that fire dragon came.

James Hill (8)
Aspley Guise Lower School

Dragon Birth

In the mountain there was some sand.
Beneath the sand there grew a snake.
Under the snake dragon was born.

Isabel Holland (9)
Aspley Guise Lower School

Dragon Birth

In the wild, wet wood there was an oak.
Beneath the oak there was a cave
And in that cave the moss crept.
Beneath the moss there was a stone.
Beneath the stone there was an egg
And in that egg there was a crack.
From that crack there was a flame.
From that flame there was a fire
And from that fire dragon came.

James Lloyd (8)
Aspley Guise Lower School

Fear

Fear is the colour red like a demon's eye.
Fear sounds like a sports car engine revving.
Fear feels like squishy play dough.
Fear reminds me of Gordon when he died.
Fear tastes like liver.
Fear smells like a freshly baked pepperoni pizza.
Fear sounds like a ghost train howling.

Taylor Gutteridge (9)
Cadmore End CE Combined School

Anger

Anger is red like blood.
Anger sounds like a thunderstorm.
Anger tastes like hot chilli peppers.
Anger smells like peppercorn being ground.
Anger looks like a blazing house fire.
Anger feels like a pain in your jaw.
Anger reminds me of very sad times.

Ashley McMahon (8)
Cadmore End CE Combined School

Fear

Fear is black like the dark.
Fear sounds like a thump on the door but no one is there!
Fear tastes like sour sea water.
Fear looks like a black hole.
Fear feels like a cold hand touching my leg.
Fear smells like rotting litter that has been left for weeks.
Fear reminds me of a flip in the belly from a ride.

Jodi Munday (9)
Cadmore End CE Combined School

Sadness

Sadness is the colour of a blue sky.
Sadness smells like a bonfire burning up to the bright clear clouds.
Sadness tastes like the snow dropping in my mouth.
Sadness looks like the sea flowing to the other side of the world.
Sadness sounds like branches tapping on my window.
Sadness feels like a tree blowing over in a storm.

Matthew Masterton (8)
Cadmore End CE Combined School

Fear

Fear is black like the darkness of midnight.
Fear feels like doom coming for me.
Fear tastes like cold snow in winter.
Fear smells like an empty black space.
Fear looks like the moon shining down on you.
Fear sounds like silence in a black room.
Fear reminds me of a roller coaster going downwards at 90mph.

Daniel Ramsdale (9)
Cadmore End CE Combined School

Sadness

Sadness is red like Remembrance poppies.
Sadness sounds like people crying.
Sadness tastes like bitter lemons.
Sadness smells like old books.
Sadness looks like grey skies.
Sadness feels like painful earache.
Sadness reminds me of my dog who died.

Millie-Isabella Ridley (8)
Cadmore End CE Combined School

Sadness

Sadness looks like a never-ending snake.
Sadness feels like a gentle breeze.
Sadness tastes like a rotten burger.
Sadness is blue like the sky.
Sadness smells like an empty space.
Sadness sounds like the blowing wind.
Sadness reminds me of a dead pet.

Jack Moorin (8)
Cadmore End CE Combined School

Sadness

Sadness is blue like tears.
Sadness sounds like a ghost town.
Sadness tastes like salty tears.
Sadness smells like old flowers.
Sadness looks like unhappy faces.
Sadness feels like a hole in your heart.
Sadness reminds me of when Pippi died.

Cameron Bates (7)
Cadmore End CE Combined School

The Dust Collector

Detailed like a newborn butterfly opening its eyes to the world
Scratched like an old abandoned car
Stained like ancient socks so comfy they're worn out and battered
That's how the world sees me.

I spend my time on a window sill collecting dust, holding nothing
With the most read book all tatty and ripped and it is loved in this household
Waiting for my turn to be used like that
That's how the world sees me.

But in my dreams I am holding jewellery for Julia Roberts
Polished and new every time someone takes a piece of bling out of me.

Spending my time watching Julia create new films for people to enjoy
as much as I do
With the bigger boxes containing her clothes
Knowing the one day that will be me
That's how I'd like to be.

Hannah Bates (10)
Cadmore End CE Combined School

Sadness

Sadness is blue like the sea.
Sadness sounds like a tree scraping on your window.
Sadness tastes like sour lemons.
Sadness smells like dead flowers.
Sadness looks like an empty room.
Sadness feels like balloons popping.
Sadness reminds me of missing someone.

Alexander Osypiw (8)
Cadmore End CE Combined School

Fear

I walked into a house
Fear seeping through me,
I stopped and I shivered,
Someone was on the couch.

I stopped and I shivered,
Wind was howling like a blizzard.

I ran up the stairs,
Stopped, still shivering,
A growling like bear's.

Into the bedroom,
Up to the loft,
To look at the shining moon.

The air was stale,
My face was pale,
Looking into the cold night.

A tickle on my back
A prickle on my feet
I was still looking into the night.

Elliot Hall (10)
Ley Hill School

Wings
(Based on 'If I Had Wings' by Pie Corbett)

If I had wings I would touch the fluffy clouds.
If I had wings I would taste the top of a roof.
If I had wings I would listen to the birds singing.
If I had wings I would smell the clean air.
If I had wings I would see the world from the sky.
If I had wings I would dream of flying in space.

James Rolfe (7)
Ley Hill School

Wings
(Based on 'If I Had Wings' by Pie Corbett)

If I had wings I would touch the moon
and come back down to Earth in three seconds.
If I had wings I would taste the ice cream candyfloss clouds
with marshmallows on top.
If I had wings I would listen to the sound of music down below me,
the sound of a band playing so nicely.
If I had wings I would smell the roses,
the sweet smell so heavenly and wonderful.
If I had wings I would gaze at the funfair
with children shouting and screaming,
Laughing as they go on fantastic rides.
If I had wings I would dream of being a bird
with the most beautiful wings ever.

Eve Gorst (7)
Ley Hill School

Wings
(Based on 'If I Had Wings' by Pie Corbett)

If I had wings I would touch the treetops of the trees in the woods.
If I had wings I would taste the water in the clouds.
If I had wings I would listen to the little robins chirping away in the
                                                          trees below.
If I had wings I would smell the lovely lavender in gardens.
If I had wings I would gaze down on the world.
If I had wings I would dream about going to Mars and eating it!

Gavin Davies (7)
Ley Hill School

Wings
(Based on 'If I Had Wings' by Pie Corbett)

If I had wings I would touch the wave of the seven seas and
                                       dolphins weaving in and out.
If I had wings I would taste the marshmallow clouds in the sky.
If I had wings I would listen to the crackle of the sun resting on the sea.
If I had wings I would smell the sweet cocoa on a tree swaying
                                       from side to side.
If I had wings I would gaze at the star resting in the light of the moon.
If I had wings I would dream of flying through space like a star
                                       and touching the rainbow.

Jamie Cullen (8)
Ley Hill School

Wings
(Based on 'If I Had Wings' by Pie Corbett)

If I had wings I would touch the snowy white fur of a polar bear.
If I had wings I would taste the floating clouds far above me.
If I had wings I would listen to the wild drill of a green woodpecker
                                       in a forest miles away.
If I had wings I would smell the gassy atmosphere of space.
If I had wings I would gaze at the feathers of a golden eagle.
If I had wings I would dream of flying to every country on Earth
                                       and back.

James Asquith (8)
Ley Hill School

Wings
(Based on 'If I Had Wings' by Pie Corbett)

If I had wings I would touch the shining emerald leaves
　　　　　　　　　　　　　　on the glimmering oak tree.
If I had wings I would taste the chocolate on Mars.
If I had wings I would listen to the rustle of the leaves far below.
If I had wings I would smell the fresh air blowing me along.
If I had wings I would gaze at the stars hanging in the sky.
If I had wings I would dream of everything that God created in the whole universe.

Ellie Pardoe (7)
Ley Hill School

Wings
(Based on 'If I Had Wings' by Pie Corbett)

If I had wings I would touch the beautiful leaves like smooth tissues.
If I had wings I would taste the lovely clouds tasting like marshmallows.
If I had wings I would listen to the birds up, up, high in the sky.
If I had wings I would smell the sweetness of the Earth.
If I had wings I would gaze at the emerald shining leaves
　　　　　　　　　　　　　　　　of a million trees.
If I had wings I would dream of stopping the people cutting down
　　　　　　　　　　　　　the rainforests and shooting animals
and the Earth would be so quiet and calm.

Aaron Taylor (7)
Ley Hill School

Wings
(Based on 'If I Had Wings' by Pie Corbett)

If I had wings I would touch the burning from the blazing sun.
If I had wings I would taste the saltiness of the fish
                                        in the Antarctic Ocean.
If I had wings I would listen to the people having fun on a beach.
If I had wings I would smell the delicious beautiful baked sausages.
If I had wings I would gaze down at the London Eye with people
                                          inside going round.
If I had wings I would dream of being in outer space and bouncing
                                              on Jupiter.

Tony Sorrenti (7)
Ley Hill School

Wings
(Based on 'If I Had Wings' by Pie Corbett)

If I had wings I would touch the warming sun getting hotter
                                          by the second.
It I had wings I would taste the finest meat in the world.
If I had wings I would listen to a shooting star and a thousand
                                          wishes wandering with it.
If I had wings I would smell the rose just before it sends its smell
                                          across the solar system.
If I had wings I would gaze out into the universe.
If I had wings I would dream of the heavens of love
                                          and the valley of life.

Mhairi Sanderson (7)
Ley Hill School

Wings
(Based on 'If I Had Wings' by Pie Corbett)

If I had wings I would touch flying birds soaring in the sky.
If I had wings I would taste the fluffy outside of the clouds.
If I had wings I would listen to the people talking on the other
                                          side of the world.
If I had wings I would smell the old smelly seaweed of the
                                          Atlantic Ocean.
If I had wings I would gaze at the hot sun only one mile away.
If I had wings I would dream of being the king of all the countries
                                          on the Earth.

Jonathan Shaw (7)
Ley Hill School

Wings
(Based on 'If I Had Wings' by Pie Corbett)

If I had wings I would touch the soft cotton clouds floating gently away.
If I had wings I would taste the marshmallows
                                    on the marshmallow tree.
If I had wings I would listen to the sea stroking the shore,
                                        as if it's stroking a cat.
If I had wings I would smell the honey which the bees are making
                                        as they buzz all around.
If I had wings I would gaze at the dolphins as they jump as high
                                as they can, far out in the blue ocean.
If I had wings I would dream of flying to the moon up and away
                                        in a rocket.

Lucia Russell (8)
Ley Hill School

Excitement

Excitement is when it's your first day of school.
Excitement is when you hear your first pet call.
Excitement is when it's your birthday, presents galore.
Excitement is when you make a new friend, you know you want more.
Excitement is sparkly.
Excitement is bright.
Excitement is the child that can't sleep tonight.
My friend, excitement is many things.

Ashley Davis (10)
Ley Hill School

Fear

Spiders crawling down your back
Tickling you in the foggy black.
Shivers run down your spine
When you see broken bottles of stale wine!

You rub your hand against the wall
It is damp; no one lives there at all.
Years have gone by
That shining speck caught your eye.

On your own, you slowly creep,
To find that treasure you so dearly seek.
To claim it as yours you would cry
But then you see something fly!

When owls hoot, you run,
The bones of people have been broken for fun!
This all builds up like a cake with cream
Suddenly you hear yourself *scream!*

Chloe Parker (10)
Ley Hill School

Wings
(Based on 'If I Had Wings' by Pie Corbett)

If I had wings I would touch the rainbow and the beautiful rainforest.
If I had wings I would taste the marshmallow clouds which are yummy.
If I had wings I would listen to the loud trumpets of Queen Elizabeth II
at Buckingham Palace in London.
If I had wings I would smell the beautiful flowers that seem tiny
                                                from up in the sky.
If I had wings I would gaze at the sunset resting on the sea
                                                which turns purple.
If I had wings I would dream of flying into Heaven to meet God
as a man and see all of my family.

Fergus Allan (7)
Ley Hill School

Fear

Fear is a feeling it's hard to get away from
Try not to have fear, it's a horrible feeling.
There is a strange house , a scary blizzard.
I'm full of fear, so scared, so frightened.
Oh so near, wolves start to howl.
I let out a scowl
For fear is gone, *for now!*

Thomas Dodd (10)
Ley Hill School

Happiness

Happiness is when Christmas comes early.
Happiness is when you pass the test.
Happiness is when the sun is out.
Happiness is when you get a new pet.

Eleanor Cooper (10)
Ley Hill School

Excitement

The joyous sound of a theme park echoes all around, excitement!
Children run around the block with a foot and one sock, excitement!
Jokes are told and your old toys are sold, excitement!
When the band is playing, people start swaying, excitement!
As you drink the caffeine the energy intervenes, excitement!
To jump on the roller coaster you feel so keen, excitement!

Matthew Berry (10)
Ley Hill School

Fear

All I can see is foggy black and lots of graves,
I smell mould and sick, I slip on a rock,
I can hear a wolf howling, he's in the distance.
Now all I can see is grey.
The moon is full, an owl hoots, I am feeling fear.

Bethany Sanderson (10)
Ley Hill School

Fury

Scratching makes me shiver.
The taste of anger is revolting,
It is like dried sick.
The colour orange boils me up.
Forks squirming on my plate.
I dislike ill-lit rooms.
That is what makes me angry.

George Loizou (10)
Ley Hill School

Excitement

Excitement is when you say your first word.
Excitement is when you walk for the first time.
Excitement is when you make your first friend.
Excitement is glittery.
Excitement is colourful.
Excitement is shiny.
Excitement is fun.
Excitement is special.
Excitement is a good feeling inside.
Excitement is when it is your birthday.
Excitement is when it is Christmas.
Excitement is when it is fireworks day.
Excitement is the best feeling in the world!

Rachel Amankwatia (10)
Ley Hill School

Happiness

I love happiness
It makes me really complete.
Friends make me jolly.
The sea is dark blue,
Red is a jolly colour,
The grass is quite green.
My dogs are quite fun,
My birthday makes me happy,
Christmas is great.

Renny King (10)
Ley Hill School

Sadness

The crystal clear tears
Make their way down my pale cheek
And it feels so cold.

You sit there waiting
For someone to notice you,
But all is silent.

Your friends feel vicious
Although they try to help you,
You start to feel ill.

Confused and upset
And the nightmare continues,
Can't anyone help?

Elleni Rogers (11)
Ley Hill School

Fear

When I'm scared I smell . . .
Mouldy, old, rotten, damp wells.
That's what I can smell.

When I'm scared I see . . .
Dark fog and mist around me.
That's what I can see.

When I'm scared I feel . . .
My spine shivers like an eel.
That's what I can feel.

Jenna Taylor (10)
Ley Hill School

Sadness

Salty tears well up in your sad eyes,
Your mouth feels sour and uncomfortable,
You can't hear anything just the boring breeze.

You've done something bad, no more than that, something *terrible!*
A massive weight rests on your shoulders, it just won't budge.
You don't feel like doing anything just hiding away on your own.

Brown, dark green, black and grey mix to form a dull sickening colour,
Everything seems to whirr around and you feel dizzy,
Suddenly you collapse!

Jennifer Davies (10)
Ley Hill School

Anger

Anger tastes like sick, mould and slime.
Anger sounds like knuckles clicking chalk on a blackboard
                                       and polystyrene breaking.
Anger feels like slugs, worms and beetles.
Anger smells like mouldy cheese and dirty fleas.
Anger looks like drowsy eyes and people not listening.
Anger is the colour black.
That's what makes me angry.

Kelsi Ellis (10)
Ley Hill School

Impatient - Haikus

Sitting on your chair,
Waiting for the bell to ring,
Will it ever go?

I am getting bored,
It is only two o'clock,
I am impatient.

Roxanne Church (10)
Ley Hill School

Wings
(Based on 'If I Had Wings' by Pie Corbett)

If I had wings I would touch the golden gates of Heaven above the sky.
If I had wings I would taste the ice cream sundae clouds.
If I had wings I would listen to the gentle breeze swooping
                                                   through the grass.
If I had wings I would smell the newborn bird in its nest.
If I had wings I would gaze at the ants dancing on the ground below.
If I had wings I would dream of flying through the sky.

Gaby Meek (8)
Ley Hill School

Fear

The graveyard is cold
You feel tickles down your back
There's a stale smell.

The streets are darkened
The graveyard is so foggy
Darkness strikes again.

All towns are pitch-black
Darkened by the misty moon
The graveyard is so damp.

Susie Crabbe (10)
Ley Hill School

Impatient

Frustrating to hold
Impatient situation
A job you can't take
Waiting for something
Red, purple, orange, yellow
I just can't take it!

Charlotte Rolfe (10)
Ley Hill School

Wings
(Based on 'If I Had Wings' by Pie Corbett)

If I had wings I would touch the light feathers of the birds.
If I had wings I would taste the fluffy cotton candy and
                                       marshmallow clouds.
If I had wings I would listen to the children playing in the
                                       playground down below me.
If I had wings I would smell the lavender-shaped clouds.
If I had wings I would gaze at the planets and stars.
If I had wings I would dream of eating Mars and balancing
                                       on the London Eye.

Dominique Puddephatt (8)
Ley Hill School

The Day The Snow Fell

In the silent night the snow fell down

S nowflakes gleaming in the night
N orway filled with layers of snow
O h snow, oh snow, oh lovely snow
W hite snow gleaming in the night sky
F ootprints in the night's snow
L akes frozen with a shiny ice
A nd people having smashing fun
K ites are blowing in the wind
E merald trees gleaming in the light
S now shining on the white frosty grass.

Nathaniel Riley (8)
St Joseph's Catholic Primary School, Chalfont St Peter

Snow

One very cold and frosty day,
That was the day,
That was the day.
The snow came!

Put on your hats,
Scarves and gloves,
Scarves and gloves.
That was the day the snow came!

Snowflakes falling,
Down, down, down,
Down, down, down.
That was the day the snow came!

Having fun, playing games,
Building snowmen,
Building snowmen.
That was the day the snow came!

Keeping warm, keeping snug
Hot chocolate,
Hot chocolate.
That was the day the snow came!

Emma Broadley (8)
St Joseph's Catholic Primary School, Chalfont St Peter

Snow

Hats and scarves,
Hats and scarves and a bubble bath.
Snow and ice,
Snow and ice falling very fast, one, two three!
Freezing cold,
Freezing cold, running very fast in the freezing cold.

Ella Maher (8)
St Joseph's Catholic Primary School, Chalfont St Peter

When The Snow Fell

S nowy snowflakes falling from the sky
N icest pies, warm as can be
O h please snow come again
W hite icicles dripping from rooftops
F iring chimneys warming my hands
L ovely roast dinners filling me up
A nd hot steamy baths
K ites whistling through the air
E xtraordinary sights from freezing mountain tops
S teaming hot chocolate ending the day.

Sean Kennedy (9)
St Joseph's Catholic Primary School, Chalfont St Peter

Snow

I looked out of the window to find some snow
It fell down to earth very slow
It was so quiet, as quiet as a mouse
As it fell onto the roof of the house
As I was getting ready to go outside
I saw my cat going to hide
She is scared of the snow
But I'm not because I know it's only snow!

Sarah Kay (9)
St Joseph's Catholic Primary School, Chalfont St Peter

Mandy

There was Mandy, Mandy
Eating all the candy
In the school
In the school.
There was Mandy, Mandy
Eating all the candy
In St Joseph's Catholic School.

Maggie O'Neill (9)
St Joseph's Catholic Primary School, Chalfont St Peter

Winter

Snowflakes falling out of the sky
So cold I have to go inside.
Hot chocolate on the stove
Drink it up before it gets cold.
Dress up warm so we can go outside
And build a snowman or have a snowball fight!
Make angels in the snow
Freezing cold so go inside!

Jessica Chapman (9)
St Joseph's Catholic Primary School, Chalfont St Peter

Snow Is Falling

Snow is falling, snow is falling,
Saying your friends' names, calling and calling.
We're having fun, we've had a bun,
We never get tired of it.
In the morning, there is no snow left, only a little bit.
I throw it up in the air,
It lands on a bear
And that is the end of the snow.

Callum Ryan (9)
St Joseph's Catholic Primary School, Chalfont St Peter

Who Made The Snow?

Squelching snow as white as can be,
But who made the snow?
Sparkling ice on the ground
But who made the ground icy?

Snowflakes exploding really fast
But who made the snowflakes?
Snowmen-building races kids do
Who makes it first and who makes it last?

Ciaran Bohan (8)
St Joseph's Catholic Primary School, Chalfont St Peter

The Day The Snow Came

The day the snow came
I was so excited and really delighted
Because it looked so white and squelchy.
So I went downstairs and had some hot chocolate,
Then I went outside to play with my hat and scarf and gloves.
Now I was really excited because I was happy to go out in the
                                              snow and play.
I was so delighted and really, really happy.

Avneet Kaur Khaira (8)
St Joseph's Catholic Primary School, Chalfont St Peter

The Snowy Day

The first drop of snow fell from the sky
While everyone inside was eating apple pie.
All the children ran outside
And Mum and Dad were all wide-eyed.

The older children had a snowball fight
But the younger children had a big fright.
The snow was crunchy, the snow was crispy
The snow was drizzling off the chimney.

But soon the snow was water
And everyone was boreder,
There were no snowflakes falling from the sky
And no one was eating apple pie.

So they went to bed
Looked out the window
And said,
'Yippee, it's snowing again!'

Stephen Moroz (9)
St Joseph's Catholic Primary School, Chalfont St Peter

The Night The Snow Came

One winter's night when I was sleeping
a silent blanket softly draped itself over the blackness.
I awoke and saw a sight I had never seen before.
A duvet of frozen crystals had crept up to our door.
The trees were no longer bare, now where there was nothing,
white leaves were there.
Our garden had no edges, no end to the sheet
that fell over the lawn and crunched under our feet.
We played all day with our new wintry friend
and then the rain came, the fun had to end.

Phoebe Roberts (8)
St Joseph's Catholic Primary School, Chalfont St Peter

The Colours Of The Seasons

Winter is white
I like Christmas
The candlelight
The snowy grass.

Spring is light green
I like hunting
For eggs outside
I sometimes hide.

Summer is blue
I like the pool
It is so cool
To swim into.

Autumn is gold
I like the leaves
Getting so old
Falling off trees.

Hortense Quazza (9)
St Joseph's Catholic Primary School, Chalfont St Peter

The Day The Snow Came

The day the snow came I could not believe it.
I looked outside and there I received it.
The snow is falling, hip hip hooray!
I must go outside to play.
I can build a snowman; I can build a tree,
I love snow 'cause it's fun for me.

Katie Schulten (9)
St Joseph's Catholic Primary School, Chalfont St Peter

In The Best Park In The World

There was Joseph, Joseph
Kicking a ball with Joey
In the park, in the park.
There was Joseph, Joseph
Kicking a ball with Joey
In the best park in the world.

Joseph Byrne (9)
St Joseph's Catholic Primary School, Chalfont St Peter

Hannah, Hannah

There was Hannah, Hannah
Playing her piano
In the school, in the school.
There was Hannah, Hannah
Playing her piano
In St Joseph's Catholic School.

Cameron Chana (9)
St Joseph's Catholic Primary School, Chalfont St Peter

Selfishness

Selfishness is a smudgy grey colour.
Selfishness tastes like a raw banana.
Selfishness is like an erupting volcano.
Selfishness looks like a grey dustbin.
Selfishness sounds like a child having a tantrum.
Selfishness feels like a knife running against your neck.

Ellie Bees (8)
St Joseph's Catholic Primary School, Chalfont St Peter

Jealousy

Jealousy is a jealousy green.
Jealousy tastes like rotten apples.
Jealousy smells like a burning candle.
Jealousy looks like an icy day.
Jealousy sounds like a rock on your head.
Jealousy feels like a disgusting rotten peach.

Elizabeth Elsworth (7)
St Joseph's Catholic Primary School, Chalfont St Peter

Love

Love is ruby-red.
Love tastes like a scarlet strawberry.
Love smells like sweet-scented roses.
Love looks like shimmering crystals.
Love sounds like wedding bells ringing out loud.
Love feels like your heart beating like a drum.

Charlotte Gilson (7)
St Joseph's Catholic Primary School, Chalfont St Peter

School Lunchtime

Lunch, lunch, lunch,
Munch, munch, munch.
I need to eat my lunch,
I like the way cucumbers crunch!

Now we are outside,
Everyone's playing tag.
None of my friends can catch me,
They all go nag, nag, nag!

The bell goes
And all the teachers yell,
'Get in your line
It's the end of playtime!'

Katie McCartney (7)
St Joseph's Catholic Primary School, Chalfont St Peter

Snowy Days

Today it's as dark as dark
Cold as cold
Snow everywhere
Freezing, freezing
Everyone is dashing around
Snowflakes are falling down
Everyone is staring and daring
While snow is falling down
Everyone is dazzling round
There is snow, snow on my bow
There is snow, snow on my bow
Everyone is having a snow fight in the moonlight
It is so dark they can't put up a fight
Goodnight!

Elena Queally (9)
St Joseph's Catholic Primary School, Chalfont St Peter

The Bench

How miserable I was!
How lonely I felt!
I had nobody to play with,
I was new to this school.

So I went to this bench,
I sat down alone.
I watched the other children
Laughing and playing.

I missed my old school
And my friends so much.
I wished I hadn't moved,
A tear rolled down my face.

Then a shadow came over me.
A boy I had never seen before
Asked me, 'Do you want to play with me?'
It was Josh, my future best friend

And these days when I pass this bench
I make sure tha nobody sits by himself.
This is my first and best memory of St Joseph's,
I will always cherish this bench.

Ladislas Quazza (10)
St Joseph's Catholic Primary School, Chalfont St Peter

Royal Hospital Bed

There was Meg, Meg
Who had a broken leg
In the bed, in the bed.

There was Meg, Meg
Who had a broken leg
In a Royal Hospital Bed.

Megan Corrigan (9)
St Joseph's Catholic Primary School, Chalfont St Peter

Snowdrops

Snowdrops everywhere
I like them and you like them
They are in a little ball and when they come up they are beautiful.
They are nice and shiny and white too.
They are all in a little row and they are delighted to be together.

Holly Daniels (7)
St Joseph's Catholic Primary School, Chalfont St Peter

Flowers

Flowers can be bought in shops
But of course we plant them in our gardens.
Summer smells of beautiful flowers growing.
They need rain and sun to make them grow.
I like to pick them because they make me glow.

Elizabeth Reeves (7)
St Joseph's Catholic Primary School, Chalfont St Peter

Football

I am football crazy
Watching it on TV makes me lazy.
Steven Gerrard on the right,
Frank Lampard takes a strike.
When he scores the goal
It raises everyone's heart and soul.
The other fans aren't so cheery,
As Ronaldo is playing very dreary.
I would like England to win the cup
Come on Ref, time must be up!
Finally the whistle blows
Will we win the cup?
Who knows!

Alex Wicks (8)
St Joseph's Catholic Primary School, Chalfont St Peter

Birthday

Soon to be my birthday, I can't wait,
I'm going to have a party; it's going to be great.
I send my invitations off in the post,
To my friends and family I like the most.
Dress up nice and be sure to have some fun,
Don't be late, the party starts at one.
Now the party's over, just me and my dog Rover.

Jessica Keyes (7)
St Joseph's Catholic Primary School, Chalfont St Peter

Happiness

Happiness is golden yellow.
Happiness tastes like juicy big bananas.
Happiness smells like gorgeous daffodils.
Happiness looks like the burning bright sun.
Happiness sounds like friends calling me.
Happiness feels like a rainbow with a pot of gold under it.

Victoria Chapman (7)
St Joseph's Catholic Primary School, Chalfont St Peter

Anger

Anger is bright red.
Anger tastes of burning steak.
Anger smells like a dragon's breath.
Anger looks like an erupting volcano.
Anger sounds like a steaming train.
Anger feels like a hissing snake.

Finlay Burrell (7)
St Joseph's Catholic Primary School, Chalfont St Peter

Sports Cars

Cars are very fast but if you go
Too fast something might come out.
Faster and faster you go,
You might get the police after you, don't do it!

A sports car is very fast
So if you get travel sick, don't go in it
Or you might be sick.
OK, come on and try it out.

I like fast cars because they *zoom, zoom, zoom!*
Do you like to go fast at all?
Come with me and we'll go to the car, car, car, show.

Callum Keane (8)
St Joseph's Catholic Primary School, Chalfont St Peter

Spring

Spring is sunny, spring is hot.
Spring is when people go on holiday.
Spring is when flowers come out.
Spring is when animals come out too.

The flowers are lovely.
The flowers are gold and rosy.
The flowers smell lovely.
The flowers grow on the lovely lime grass.

The animals start coming out.
The animals start playing in the sunshine.
The frogs are hopping in the river.
The rabbits are bouncing and hopping about.

Ciara Hildrew (8)
St Joseph's Catholic Primary School, Chalfont St Peter

The Battle

There goes Ronaldo running down the line
Who crosses the ball to Rooney who smashes it across the line.
It's one-nil to United!
The fans are going mad
Hearts are thumping, cheeks are red.
Running up and down the pitch,
Trying to stay ahead.
United on the attack again,
The fans are cheering.
A few minutes to go
The ref blows his whistle,
The fans are going wild.
Full time!
Phew!

Charlie Harrison (7)
St Joseph's Catholic Primary School, Chalfont St Peter

Dance

When you first put your feet on the dance floor
You feel like a dancing diva!
The music is so loud,
It could damage someone's ears
And give them a fever.

So I think it's time you too knew
What type of dance we do . . .
We are tripping and jumping across the floor like a ballerina
And some people are even doing the jig and wearing a wig.

We prance across the floor all the way to the door.
We have such a good time when we dance
So we hope you will dance with us next time.

Evie Vennix (7)
St Joseph's Catholic Primary School, Chalfont St Peter

The Missing Chocolate Bar

I swear I didn't eat it
The dog ate it so don't blame me.
Of course I couldn't, I was at the park
And while I was there I was listening to a dog bark.
Then later on that day I went to the shop
And went to the counter to buy a lollipop.
I didn't eat the chocolate bar; it was mud on my face
So don't think it was me just in case!

Amy Werrell (9)
St Mary's Wavendon CE Primary School, Wavendon

Snow

Snow can be soft, snow can be hard
Snow can be anywhere at all.
Snow can fall heavy, snow can fall light
Snow can fall anywhere at all.
Snow is fun to play with anywhere and any time.

Ruby Lockyer (7)
St Mary's Wavendon CE Primary School, Wavendon

Cars

C ars, fast and slow
A lfa Romeo I think is quite fast
R ubbish cars are Morris Minors
S uper cars are my favourite.

Kieran Gissane (10)
St Mary's Wavendon CE Primary School, Wavendon

How Are You?

Dad can't see why I get bored of him saying, 'How are you?'
He tuts and rolls his eyes to all of my replies . . .
Stressed
Not well
Angry
Bored
Fine
OK
Good
Grubby
Cool!
Useless
But sometimes I don't answer!
It does really annoy me
But at the end of the day he is part of the family so
                        I might as well love him.

Liberty Bowler (10)
St Mary's Wavendon CE Primary School, Wavendon

Romans

Julius Caesar
The Roman geezer
Came to Britain
Was not smitten
Back to Gaul
After all.

Jake Poyner (10)
St Mary's Wavendon CE Primary School, Wavendon

Animals

Animals are cute and furry
Some animals are curvy
A lot of animals have big eyes
Dogs don't like pie
Birds build a nest
Monkeys are pests
Horses run fast
Frogs cannot wear a cast
Cats eat fish
Dogs prefer dog food in a dish
The tigers are out getting food
Lucky for you they're in a good mood
Fish like to have a swim
Gorillas like the gym
Foxes hunt animals
Crows are cannibals.

Courtney McAloon (9)
St Mary's Wavendon CE Primary School, Wavendon

Mountains

Mountains are the king of ice
And they are fairly nice
The tips are topped with snow
And it has a cold, clear river flow.
Mount Everest there may be, they will always be seen.

Naveen Mahil (10)
Stoke Poges School

April

April is my birthday
Easter, lots of eggs for me
April is a special type of month
April.

Sophie Jones (10)
Stoke Poges School

One Old Oily Ox

One old oily ox on an obstacle course.
Two tremendous terrible T-rex fighting.
Three terrible turtles trying to turn on their backs.
Four flapping fish are frying in a pan.
Five flying finches flying in the air.
Six slithering snakes having a snack.
Seven secret sharks swimming after fish.
Eight enormous elephants eating an egg.
Nine naughty nurses nibbling tasty nuggets.
Ten thirsty tigers trying to taste their tea.

Morgan Pitt (7)
Stoke Poges School

Limerick

There once was a bird who fluttered,
He fell in his coffee and spluttered,
'I'm scorching my feet
And losing my tweet.'
But nobody heard because he muttered.

Haris Malik (11)
Stoke Poges School

Teacher

Homework marker
Coffee drinker
Top educator
Board writer
Child minder
Human dictionary
Whistle blower
Rule keeper
Nose wiper.

Jonathan Schondorfer (11)
Stoke Poges School

In The Bedroom

In the bedroom
It was shiny,
No dust, no rubbish,
But glittery and clean.

Some stuff is in piles,
Some is under the bed,
Some is in cupboards,
Some is in drawers.

My walls are golden,
The paint is red,
The wallpaper is silver,
The clock is pink and blue.

Nikita Sanan (7)
Stoke Poges School

My Hamster

I have a hamster
His name is Monkey.
He is very special to me.
I got him when he was a baby.
He runs in his ball
He sometimes runs into the wall.
He loves treats
That's why he is special to me.

Taylor Nelmes (10)
Stoke Poges School

Chocolate

Chocolate is tasty,
I could have it for dinner
But then I'll get bigger.
So what shall I do?
Should I have it all
Or just a little bit?
Hmmm, what shall I do?
I can feel the taste in my mouth
Is it Mars or just chocolate bars?
Oh I'll just have it all
Mmm, yummy, oh Mummy
I think I'm going to be sick.
From now on it's just plain carrot sticks.

Ryanvir Lalli (10)
Stoke Poges School

Primates

I love the sound of monkeys,
Gibbons, apes and chimps,
All of these are primates,
The best animals in the world!

Monkeys aren't just brown,
They're orange, white and black,
If you mess with a monkey
Then you will get a smack!

Munisah Rasheed (10)
Stoke Poges School

Ten Scientists

Ten scientists standing in a line, one got an idea then there were nine.
Nine scientists chatting with a mate, one ran away
                                         then there were eight.
Eight scientists researching Devon, one retired then there were seven.
Seven scientists eating Weetabix, one vomited then there were six.
Six scientists at the beach, one wouldn't drive then there were five.
Five scientists eating apples, one swallowed the core
                                         then there were four.
Four scientist riding bikes to test drag, one hurt his knee
                                         then there were three,
Three scientists drinking tea and eating cake, one couldn't chew
                                         then there were two.
Two scientists went for a run, one got lost then there was one.
One scientist did a test, once he was done there were none.

Zishan Hussain (10)
Stoke Poges School

The Marine

A scope shooter
A man manoeuvre
A fearless fighter
A gutsy gunner
A trained terminator
An expert eliminator
What am I?
I am a marine.

Qasar Ali (10)
Stoke Poges School

An Elephant In The City

An elephant in the city
Have you ever heard such rubbish?
He crushed a car
Oh what a pity!

A kangaroo in the Arctic
Have you ever heard such a hullabaloo?
He booked a flight back to Australia,
'Oh well,' he said, 'I will be back home in a millisec!'

A pig in the rainforest
Have you ever heard such nonsense?
He drowned in a river
Oh no, that is the horriblest!

A human caged in the zoo
Have you ever heard such a story?
He just couldn't cope
Oh dear, what should he do!

Stephanie Matthews (10)
Stoke Poges School

Zonda

There was a great car called a Zonda
Who hated his rival named Honda.
They had a big crash,
And ended in trash,
And were carted off to the Rhonda.

Nathan Saggar (10)
Stoke Poges School

Excitement

Excitement is multicoloured.
It smells like fresh air.
Excitement tastes like fizzy candy.
It sounds like popping popcorn.
Excitement is bouncy and joyful.
It lives in the heart of everyone.

Katie Oakley (10)
Stoke Poges School

April - Cinquain

April
Is my birthday.
Easter brings lots of eggs
April does mean the world to me
April.

Elliot Lowe (10)
Stoke Poges School

Summer

Summer has gone
Winter is here
All the frosty and cold nights are here
So go outside or come in
Summer.

Carol-Anne Smith (10)
Stoke Poges School

What Is My Pet?

My pet can walk on four legs.
My pet has black stripes.
My pet can camouflage.
My pet is a meat-eater.
My pet is a killer.
My pet stalks his prey.
What is my pet?

Fleur Cunningham (10)
Stoke Poges School

Hope

Hope is bright orange.
It smells like sweet tulips.
Hope feels like soft marshmallows.
It tastes like sweets.
It sounds like children talking.
Hope lives in everyone.

Rebecca Iona-Smith (10)
Stoke Poges School

Joy

Joy is red.
It smells like lavender air freshener.
Joy tastes like a sweet pure of coconut.
It sounds like an echo of your voice.
It feels sweet and sensitive.
Joy lives deep in your heart.

Ryan Kullar (10)
Stoke Poges School

Sea Animals

Dolphins glide through the water,
Gracefully leap in the air.
They swim around happily
Having fun without a care!

Jellyfish swim through the water,
Sometimes quite near the shore.
If you play in the water
You could get quite sore.

Sharks lurk in the water,
They swim around quietly.
If you're not careful you'll get eaten
So I'd get out if it were me.

Abigail Duck (10)
Stoke Poges School

Happiness

Happiness is blue.
It smells like roasted marshmallows.
Happiness tastes like melted chocolate.
It sounds like people laughing.
Happiness feels like soft velvet.
Happiness lives deep down in the soul.

Sophie Brown (10)
Stoke Poges School

Summer - Cinquain

Summer,
Hot day, clear sky
Floating on the water.
Diving deeply in the calm sea,
Perfect!

Amelia Edwards (10)
Stoke Poges School

Pain

Pain is the colour of tears.
It smells like the breath of a tiger.
It sounds like you're screaming for help.
It feels like you're alone in the park.
It lives inside ready to blast the pain of a volcano.

Nathan Allen (10)
Stoke Poges School

Limerick

There once was a teacher called Terry,
Who never had more than a penny.
He spent all his money,
On apples and honey
And had the best ride on a ferry.

Jade Riley (10)
Stoke Poges School

Our Teacher

A mind reader
A brain teaser
A child minder
A test timer
A star-time taker
A homework maker
A number one educator
A fast coffee drinker
That is our teacher.

Cindy Sidhu (10)
Stoke Poges School

I Wish I Was On My Own

I wish I was on my own
To do what I want, to be free
I wish I was on my own.

But being on your own comes with a down side
You have to find shelter and food.
I wish I was on my own to do what I want
Without having my mum and dad shouting.
I wish I was on my own.

Charlie Hall (10)
Stoke Poges School

Chocolate

Chocolate is creamy.
Chocolate is sweet.
Chocolate is yummy in your tummy.
Chocolate is delicious.
Chocolate is dark.
Chocolate is white.
Chocolate is hard.
Chocolate is soft.
Chocolate is sticky
And bad for your teeth!

Amie Pearce (10)
Stoke Poges School

The Mole

There is a mole
Who lives in a hole,
He has no friends,
His tunnel never ends
That poor mole with no soul.

Poppy Stevens (10)
Stoke Poges School

What Is A Tuka-Makakha?

What is a tuka-makakha?
Is it a bird? Is it a plane?
Is it big? Is it small?
What is a tuka-makakha?
Is a tuka-makakha, colourful or plain
Or is a tuka-makakha fat or thin?
Can a tuka-makakha be a . . .
Bird
Plane
Big
Small
Colourful
Plain
Fat
Thin?
What is a tuka-makakha?

Crispin Imani (9)
Stoke Poges School

My Pet

My pet doesn't have fins.
My pet doesn't have four feet.
My pet isn't pink
And doesn't have a curly tail.
My pet hasn't got a mane.
My pet is a squawking parrot!

Sally Hearn (9)
Stoke Poges School

The Shark - Haiku

Swimming silently
Looking for prey to devour.
Closing in its jaws.

Arjan Singh Grewal (9)
Stoke Poges School

My Grandad

My grandad is the best,
I love him every day.
He died when I was small,
Now he's far away.

My grandad used to play with me,
We always had a rest.
He's always my number one
And the very best!

My grandad is a star,
I miss him every day.
He always gave me cuddles,
I just wanted him to stay.

I really miss my grandad,
He really is far,
He kept me in his hands
But now he's in the stars.

Megan Wicks (9)
Stoke Poges School

Guess My Pet

My pet doesn't live underwater.
My pet can't fly.
My pet doesn't have scales or wings.
My pet's got lots of hair.
My pet doesn't live in the desert or the North Pole.
My pet goes 'woof, woof' all the time.
Can you guess my pet?

Gurneet Dhanoa (10)
Stoke Poges School

Leaping Lizards

Ten leaping lizards basking in a line,
One burnt its nose then there were nine.
Nine komodo dragons getting ready to wait,
One found food and then there were eight.
Eight blue-tongued skunks complaining about Devon,
One moved there and then there were seven.
Seven green iguanas eating Weetabix,
One was too soggy and then there were six.
Six cool chameleons going for a dive,
One suddenly drown and then there were five.
Five green geckos' feet were getting sore,
One went red and then there were four.
Four mean monitors ready to go and flee,
One stopped dead and then there were three.
Three lively slowworms ready to meet you,
One climbed up my trousers and then there were two.
Two leaping lizards basking in the sun,
One ran away then there was one.
One learning lizard thinking he was done,
He got some more work and then there were none!

Sophia Young (9)
Stoke Poges School

Up In The Attic

(Read this poem from the bottom up. It's good to be different!)

With old tattered tags
Old rusty bags
And rusty old rugs
Creepy-crawly bugs
Wobbly old chairs
Soft teddy bears
Up in the attic . . .

Charlotte Hough (9)
Stoke Poges School

Hailstones

A hailstone is white.
It smells plain and simple.
It tastes like cold, frosty ice.
It sounds like it's banging on the roof.
It feels so cold you can't touch it.
It lives up high in the clouds in the sky.

Simran Bains (9)
Stoke Poges School

Happiness

Happiness is rosy red.
It smells like sweet roses.
Happiness tastes of luscious chocolates.
It sounds like children singing brilliantly.
It feels like the biggest, comfiest bed.
Happiness lives in the centre of the sun.

Hemma Jalif (9)
Stoke Poges School

My Pet

My pet is very slithery.
My pet is very smooth.
My pet is quite dangerous
And my pet spits venom.
Can you guess what my pet is?
It's a snake, it's a snake!

Qais Ased Ali (9)
Stoke Poges School

Chocolate

Chocolate can be brown.
Chocolate can be white.
Chocolate is delicious.
Chocolate is nice.
Chocolate is tasty.
Chocolate is yummy.
Chocolate may be addictive
So you'd better watch out!

Aisha Manzoor (9)
Stoke Poges School

Love Is Red

It smells like a rose.
It tastes like a chocolate river.
It sounds like a harp playing.
It feels like a heart pounding.
Love is in your heart.

Sophie Francis (9)
Stoke Poges School

Snow

Snow is like white candyfloss.
It smells like fresh roses.
Snow tastes like an ice lolly.
It sounds like children playing.
It is soft and lovely.
Snow lives in the sky.

Jasneet Badyal (9)
Stoke Poges School

My Beach

This is not any sort of beach, this is *my* beach
Where the waves clash against the bright yellow sand
Smoothing the sandcastles wherever they stand.
This is not any sort of beach, this is *my* beach.
It has shells of crystal, bronze, silver and gold,
Warm breeze passes as the days unfold.
This is not any sort of beach, this is *my* beach.
High cliffs shining as the sun turns red,
My favourite view to see before I go to bed.
This is not any sort of beach, this is *my* beach.

Aisha Afzal (9)
Stoke Poges School

Summer

Summer is warm then babies are born.
Skylarks are flying in the cool breeze.
The sun is in the air
Primroses sway in the breezes, so do cornflowers.
Cows eating daisies in fields.
Children swing in the park.
Blossom in the breeze.
Kids eating ice cream everywhere.

Matthew Devine (9)
Stoke Poges School

One Orange Octopus

One orange octopus offering oysters.
Two tigers trying to take their tables.
Three talking turtles drinking tea.
Four frightened foxes freezing their fur off.
Five funny Frenchmen fishing for food.

Bethany Johnson (8)
Stoke Poges School

Food

Ice cream, jelly and custard,
I don't like spicy mustard.
I love mozzarella cheese,
I don't like vegetables like peas.
I love fish and chips
But chilli sauce burns my lips.
Lots and lots of sweets,
Sour rice paper sheets.
Most of all I like Mars
Especially the ones that come in bars!

Amrita Heer (8)
Stoke Poges School

My Brother And Sister

My sister is cute,
My brother is alright,
My sister's wicked,
My brother's a sight.
Sisters, sisters,
Brothers, brothers,
I play with them all night.

Danni Wylie (9)
Stoke Poges School

I Love Multiplication

I love multiplication
'Cause it's a sensation!
And if you know
Your twelve times table
You'll get a sticker with a label.

Azure Jamali (8)
Stoke Poges School

One Old Octopus

One octopus playing on a box with an old ox.
Two twirling turtles teaching a test.
Three tidy thieves tickling a teddy.
Four flippers on a fish with a dish.
Five flying fish with a fake fox.
Six stupid snakes slithering through the supermarket.
Seven sandy squirrels singing softly.
Eight elves eating an enormous egg.
Nine naughty nuns nibbling nuggets with nuts.
Ten twinkling twins taking turns to trampoline.

Shakeel Pathmanadan (8)
Stoke Poges School

One Old Ox

One old ox on an obstacle course.
Two terrible turtles trotting to town.
Three tiny toads trying to jump.
Four frightful foxes frying four fish.
Five fierce finches flying forward fast.
Six silly snakes slithering silently.
Seven stupid sharks swimming after shrimps.
Eight excited eagles eating elephants.
Nine naked nannies nibbling nuggets.
Ten terrible tractor drivers trying to have a Tango.

Robert Bagge (8)
Stoke Poges School

One Old Ox

One old ox on an obstacle course.
Two terrible turtles trying to tickle.
Three tiny toads trying to jump.
Four frightening foxes fighting ferocious fish.
Five footballers in a football stadium.
Six slimy slugs in silver shells.
Seven slithering snakes swimming swiftly.
Eight eagles eating elephants.
Nine naughty bees eating nectar.
Ten twirling tigers twisting everywhere.

Harley Dyer (7)
Stoke Poges School

One Old Ox

One old ox on an obstacle course.
Two terrible turtles trying to turn.
Three terrible tarantulas tidying up.
Four fierce frankfurters frying in a pan.
Five thirsty tigers thundering in the trees.
Six sizzling sausages.
Seven slithering snakes sliding through the grass.
Eight enormous elephants eating eggs.
Nine naughty newts nibbling nuts.
Ten tickling towers trying to eat tea.

Josh Stevenson (7)
Stoke Poges School

One Orange Octopus

One orange octopus in the ocean.
Two tall turtles in a terrible temper.
Three thirsty tigers tasting some Turkish Delight.
Four fighting fish frying in a pan.
Five fairies flying with their families.
Six sad sailors sailing to sea.
Seven slimy snakes singing to school.
Eight enormous elephants celebrating Eid.
Nine naughty nannies taking a nap.
Ten tall tap dancers tapping through town.

Hanaa Is-haq (7)
Stoke Poges School

Paint! Paint! Paint!

Paint on the ceiling.
Paint in my hair.
Paint on my apron.
Paint on the chair.
Paint all around me.
Paint everywhere except on my paper
There's no paint there!

Simran-Jaya Buttar (8)
Stoke Poges School

Little Boy Blue

This is a rap about Little Boy Blue
He went to the doctors and had the flu.
Then a cow scared him with a big moo
And that cured his flu.

Iwan Arden (7)
Stoke Poges School

One Old Octopus

One old octopus oozing on an organic orange.
Two triangular tubes trying to take-off together.
Three tiny tadpoles doing a temporary tender tennis task.
Four fat familiar famous firemen firing fat chunks of water.
Five fantastic fair farmers folding warm sheets.
Six scruffy snakes snapping and sharpening their smooth teeth.
Seven stockings standing sideways saying, 'When is supper?'
Eight eels entering Europe.
Nine naughty nuggets nosing around nicely.
Ten twirly, tiny, twisty trollies talking about twisting.

Laura Woolhouse (7)
Stoke Poges School

Whisky

Whisky is the name of my cat, she is soft and fluffy and rather fat.
She drinks lots of milk and eats lots of food which puts her
                              in a really good mood.
She climbs up trees and chases mice but I love my cat,
                              she's so very nice.

Alexa Van Deelen (7)
Stoke Poges School

One Orange Octopus

One orange octopus offending oysters.
Two trackers trying to trace tiny tigers.
Three twinkling twits twitching.
Four flipping fishes frying in a pan.
Five flicking fairies flapping their wings.

Gareth Forward (7)
Stoke Poges School

Ten Terrible Giants

Ten terrible giants toppling and tumbling terribly.
Nine naughty giants eating fried French people.
Eight evil giants eating Estonian eagles.
Seven sly giants slurping Slovakian soup.
Six silly giants swallowing spiky Spanish spindles.
Five funny giants farting fearsome farts.
Four foolish giants frying Finnish tarts.
Three thoughtful giants thinking thunderous thoughts.
Two titchy giants tucking into tea.
One giant left, I hope he doesn't eat me!

Max Nowers (8)
Stoke Poges School

Naughty Children

Ten naughty children standing on a line,
One lost his balance then there were nine.
Nine naughty children going through the gate,
One was ill then there were eight.
Eight naughty children going to Devon,
One didn't pay then there were seven.
Seven naughty children eating sticky Twix,
One didn't like it then there were six.
Six naughty children going for a drive,
One couldn't fit in the car then there were five.
Five naughty children rocking on a door,
One got caught then there were four.
Four naughty children climbing up a tree,
One fell off then there were three.
Three naughty children going to the loo,
One didn't have to go then there were two.
Two naughty children having lots of fun
One went home then there was one.
One naughty child having some Aero,
He finished it all then there were zero.

Khayam Khalid (9)
Stoke Poges School

Ten Mad Cats

Ten mad cats going to the shops,
One cat saw a sign then there were nine.
Nine mad cats going to a fête,
One burnt his toast then there were eight.
Eight mad cats being little terrors,
One went to Heaven then there were seven.
Seven mad cats eating fried Twix,
One burnt his bottom then there were six.
Six mad cats looking at a hive,
One got blind then there were five.
Five mad cats going to a war
One hurt his paw then there were four.
Four mad cats climbing up a tree,
One got stung by a bee then there were three.
Three mad cats eating some fish,
One said moo then there were two.
Two mad cats having some tea,
One lost a tooth then there was one.
One mad cat sleeping in the sun,
It never woke up then there were none.

Aisha Anwar (9)
Stoke Poges School

Chelsea

Chelsea are the best
They can beat all the rest
We have got Drogba
Boulahrouz, he is a fouler
Lampard, he can hit one
Terry that can head one
Cech has got a rugby hat
All that I can think of is Chelsea winning everything!
Come on you blues!

Aaron Fetherston (10)
Stoke Poges School

One Old Octopus

One old octopus on an obstacle course.
Two twitching turtles trying to sing.
Three tough tigers trying to fight.
Four flying birds flapping their wings.
Five fierce finches going forward fast.
Six silly snakes snacking on seven shrimp.
Seven sizzling sausages.
Eight excited elephants eating fried egg.
Nine nannies nibbling nuggets.
Ten turkeys tapping their feet.

Matthew Scott (7)
Stoke Poges School

Meeting Happiness

I met Happiness,
Her laugh is like tinkling bells,
She wore a skirt made of silk,
She smiled; she put her thin hand on her chest.

I followed her to Sadness,
She comforted him like always,
Then glided back to her garden.

She went to the lake where Lonely always sat,
She asked if he would play with her
Then laughed her tinkling bells again.
It echoed through the grasslands,
If Happiness ever died,
So would everybody with a good mind.

Natalie Pound (9)
Swanbourne House School

Young Writers Information

We hope you have enjoyed reading this book - and that you will continue to enjoy it in the coming years.

If you like reading and writing poetry drop us a line, or give us a call, and we'll send you a free information pack.

Alternatively if you would like to order further copies of this book or any of our other titles, then please give us a call or log onto our website at www.youngwriters.co.uk

Young Writers Information
Remus House
Coltsfoot Drive
Peterborough
PE2 9JX

(01733) 890066